NATIVE
AMERICANS

NEZ PERCE

Big Buddy Books

An Imprint of Abdo Publishing
www.abdopublishing.com

Sarah Tieck

www.abdopublishing.com

Published by Abdo Publishing, a division of ABDO, PO Box 398166, Minneapolis, Minnesota 55439.
Copyright © 2015 by Abdo Consulting Group, Inc. International copyrights reserved in all countries. No part
of this book may be reproduced in any form without written permission from the publisher. Big Buddy Books™
is a trademark and logo of Abdo Publishing.

Printed in the United States of America, North Mankato, Minnesota.
102014
012015

Cover Photo: ASSOCIATED PRESS; Shutterstock.com.
Interior Photos: © NativeStock.com/Angel Wynn (pp. 5, 9, 11, 13, 15, 16, 17, 23, 25, 26, 27, 29, 30); Shutterstock.com
    (pp. 19, 21).

Coordinating Series Editor: Rochelle Baltzer
Contributing Editors: Megan M. Gunderson, Marcia Zappa
Graphic Design: Adam Craven

Library of Congress Cataloging-in-Publication Data

Tieck, Sarah, 1976-
  Nez Perce / Sarah Tieck.
      pages cm. -- (Native Americans)
  Audience: Ages 7-11.
  ISBN 978-1-62403-582-1
  1. Nez Perce Indians--Juvenile literature. I. Title.
  E99.N5T54 2015
  979.5004'974124--dc23
                          2014029818

CONTENTS

Amazing People

Hundreds of years ago, North America was mostly wild, open land. Native American tribes lived on the land. They had their own languages and customs.

The Nez Perce (NEHZ PUHRS) are one Native American tribe. They are known for their fishing skills and religious beliefs. Let's learn more about these Native Americans.

Did You Know?

The name *Nez Perce* means "pierced nose." Some Nez Perce nose piercings were unusual and striking. But few people actually had them.

Modern Nez Perce teach others about their people's way of life. Appaloosa horses have been important to the tribe for many years.

Nez Perce Territory

Nez Perce homelands were in what is now Idaho, Oregon, and Washington. The tribe lived on **plateaus** near the Snake, Salmon, and Clearwater Rivers. Today, many Nez Perce live in Idaho and Washington.

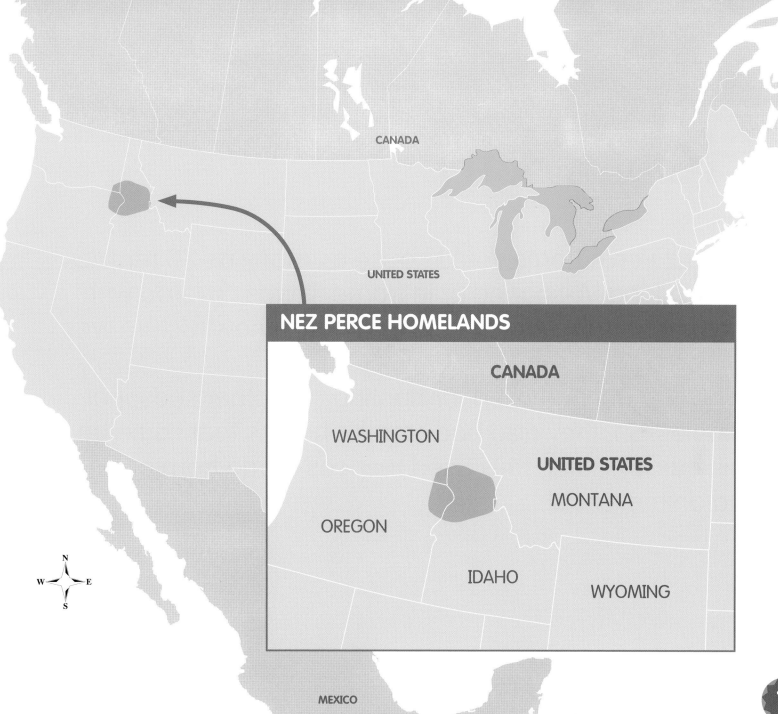

NEZ PERCE HOMELANDS

CANADA

UNITED STATES

WASHINGTON

UNITED STATES

MONTANA

OREGON

IDAHO

WYOMING

N
W E
S

MEXICO

Home Life

A Nez Perce home could house as many as 30 families. It had a long, A-shaped pole frame. It was covered with mats made from dried grass and bark. The structure was built on a pit.

The Nez Perce moved for hunting and other seasonal activities. So, they also had smaller homes that could be built quickly. Later, they used teepees made from poles and animal skins.

Much of the year, the Nez Perce lived in large mat dwellings.

What They Ate

The Nez Perce were skilled fishers. They caught salmon in rivers and streams. They also hunted elk, deer, and later, buffalo.

The Nez Perce spent a lot of time gathering plants. These included onions, carrots, berries, nuts, seeds, and camas bulbs.

Sometimes, it was hard to find food on the high, dry land. So, the tribe moved to different places in search of food. They also dried and stored extra food.

The Nez Perce used spears (*above*), nets, and traps to catch fish. They dried the fish they caught (*left*).

DAILY LIFE

The Nez Perce lived in small villages. Villages were often near salmon streams. This made chores such as fishing easier.

Nez Perce men wore moccasins, leggings, fringed buckskin shirts, and gloves. They wore fur robes to stay warm in winter. Women wore buckskin dresses, basket hats, and moccasins that went to their knees.

The Nez Perce decorated their clothes with colorful beads.

In a Nez Perce village, people worked together to survive. Men were chiefs, storytellers, healers, fishers, and hunters. They trained and cared for horses. They also fought to keep their land and families safe.

Women took care of the children and ran the homes. They gathered plants and dug up root vegetables. They also dried salmon for the tribe's food. Some women were storytellers, healers, and artists. Children learned by helping and watching others in the community.

Mothers and elders played an important part in raising children. Elders taught them the Nez Perce way of life.

MADE BY HAND

The Nez Perce made many objects by hand. They often used natural materials. These arts and crafts added beauty to everyday life.

Jewelry

The Nez Perce were named for shell bead decorations in their noses. They made other types of jewelry using glass beads, elk teeth, and bone tubes. They sometimes traded with other tribes for new materials.

Rawhide Painting

The Nez Perce made bags and other items from rawhide. Then, they painted colorful patterns on them. They used rawhide bags to carry things. They also traded them for other supplies.

Musical Instruments

Music was important to the Nez Perce. They made many instruments. The Nez Perce played flutes during rituals. They often danced to drums and rattles.

Spirit Life

The Nez Perce religion had special **ceremonies** and **rituals**. It was closely tied to nature. People also believed they had guardian spirits.

Singing and dancing was important to the Nez Perce. The Guardian Spirit Dance is a ceremony held in winter. Young people sing and dance to connect with their guardian spirits. The tribe also had war dances to prepare for battle.

Life was often dangerous for the Nez Perce. They had to cross rivers or fight others. They prayed to their guardian spirits for protection and help.

STORYTELLERS

Stories are important to the Nez Perce. Men and women told stories to their people. The stories shared the tribe's **culture**, land, and history.

Some Nez Perce legends are about characters, such as Coyote. Stories about Ant and Yellowjacket and the Heart of the Monster are about special places.

In stories, Coyote is sometimes a trickster.

Fighting for Land

It is believed the Nez Perce **descended** from people who moved to the area around 10,000 to 5500 BC. The Nez Perce settled high on a **plateau**.

In the early 1700s the Nez Perce got horses. This changed their lifestyle. They became more interested in war. They began to expand their territory. They learned from the **plains** tribes and hunted buffalo. And, they began to breed a kind of horse called the Appaloosa.

 Appaloosa horses are known for their spotted coats.

In the 1800s, American settlers arrived on Nez Perce land. In 1855, the US government set aside a large reservation for the tribe.

By the 1860s, gold had been discovered and settlers wanted more land. So, the US government took away much of the tribe's land.

The Nez Perce fought to keep their land. In the late 1800s, Chief Joseph led this fight. He and other Nez Perce fought for their homelands and way of life.

Chief Joseph's Nez Perce name was In-mut-too-yah-lat-lat. It means "thunder rolling down the mountains."

Back in Time

1805

Explorers Meriwether Lewis and William Clark became the first Americans to meet the Nez Perce.

Before 1800s

The Nez Perce started the Appaloosa breed of horses. They had some of North America's largest horse herds.

WELCOME TO WEIPPE

WHERE THE NEZ PERCE INDIANS MET LEWIS & CLARK IN 1805

Early 1700s

The Nez Perce got their first horses.

1855

The US government set up a Nez Perce reservation. It included most of their traditional homelands.

1877

Chief Joseph and the Nez Perce fought the US government at the Battle of Bear Paw Mountains. Many surrendered. They were sent to Indian Territory in what is now Oklahoma.

1996

The Nez Perce returned to the Wallowa Valley. It had been many years since this special part of their homelands had belonged to the tribe.

The Nez Perce Today

   The Nez Perce have a long, rich history. They are remembered for their decorated clothing and Appaloosa horses.

   Nez Perce roots run deep. Today, the people have kept alive those special things that make them Nez Perce. Even though times have changed, many people carry the **traditions**, stories, and memories of the past into the present.

Did You Know?

In 2010, there were about 3,700 Nez Perce people living in the United States.

Feather fans and peace pipes are part of Nez Perce traditional outfits.

"Let me be a free man–free to travel, free to stop, free to work, free to trade where I choose, free to choose my own teachers, free to follow the religion of my fathers, free to think and talk and act for myself–and I will obey every law, or submit to the penalty."

— Chief Joseph

Glossary

ceremony a formal event on a special occasion.

culture (KUHL-chuhr) the arts, beliefs, and ways of life of a group of people.

custom a practice that has been around a long time and is common to a group or a place.

descend (dih-SEHND) to be distantly related to.

plains flat or rolling land without trees.

plateau (pla-TOH) a raised area of flat land.

reservation (reh-zuhr-VAY-shuhn) a piece of land set aside by the government for Native Americans to live on.

ritual (RIH-chuh-wuhl) a formal act or set of acts that is repeated.

surrender to give up.

tradition (truh-DIH-shuhn) a belief, a custom, or a story handed down from older people to younger people.

Websites

To learn more about Native Americans, visit **booklinks.abdopublishing.com**. These links are routinely monitored and updated to provide the most current information available.

31

INDEX

DATE DUE